Common Sense & Coffee

What I've Learned & Want You to Know

By Angel K. Robinson

Author: Angel K. Robinson

© 2017 by Angel K. Robinson

All rights reserved. No part of this book may be reproduced in any form or by any means without prior written permission from the publisher, except for brief quotations used in reviews written specifically for inclusion in a magazine, newspaper, or broadcast media.

Design: Angel K. Robinson and Jennifer Shermer Pack
Layout: Jennifer Shermer Pack
Editorial Consultant: Monica Kelley

Printed in The United States of America

ISBN:
(10 digit)   1546843590
(13 digit)   978-1546843597

To Deborah,
My favorite pillow goddess!
Best,
Angel K. Robinson

For my mama, my endless source of common sense wisdom.

And to my 6th grade self, who first dreamed of seeing her name in print, WE DID IT!!!!

9	Cultivate Your Own Style
11	Everyone Creates Their Own Truth
13	Speak the Truth or Don't Speak
15	Make Big Plans
17	Don't Practice the Wrong Technique
19	Know Better. Do Better. Repeat.
21	What Brings You Joy?
23	NOW is the new Janaury
25	Savor the Good Memories
27	Self-doubt is not a Friend
29	Calm Down
31	Today is a Good Day No Matter What
33	Be Yourself
35	Bake a New Cake
37	Be Overwhelmed by Gratitude
39	Write More. Text Less.
41	I Think I Can
43	Think the Next Thought
45	Celebrate Your Opposites
47	Forgive Before the Fight
49	Get A Hobby
51	Your Voice Has Value
53	Don't do Wrong Just Because it's Fun
55	The Next Thought Never counts More than the Action
57	Yes you know, But Do You Understand?

59	It's Okay to Have a Fit for a Little Bit
61	You Have to Impress No One
63	Actions Never Leave Home Without Consequences
65	Say "I Love You"
67	Credit is Not Necessary
69	You're Awesome. Believe it.
71	Boredom is a Choice
73	Cultivate Curiousity
75	Cherish Old Friends
77	Don't Bury Your Dreams
79	Complaining is not a Strategy
81	Save Yourself
83	Fail Sometimes
85	We are the same. Our experiences are different.
87	A Zebra is not a Horse
89	Smile
91	Truth Outweighs Feelings
93	Keep Moving
95	You Can't Expect Whole Love from a Broken Person
97	Trust Your Talent
99	Keep Your Light On
101	Done is Better than Perfect
103	Learn Your Instrument
105	If you want the fruit, take responsibility for the tree.
107	Success is Built in Practice

Introduction

My favorite time of day is the last few moments before the sun rises. It is in that time, I gather my coffee mug, a notebook and pen, and sit in my quiet, dark kitchen writing while enjoying the familiar smell of old school New Orleans coffee and chicory. It is my time to think, to dream, to reminisce, and most importantly, to prepare my intention for the day.

For many years, I wrote solely for myself. I've been writing in journals since I was 15 years old. Of all the material things I lost in Hurricane Katrina in 2005, saying goodbye to all my journals, hurt the most. It took me a long time to begin writing again. The loss was too painful. Eventually, I realized that I had to write to get back to the heart of myself. My soul needed it. So I started my old ritual of writing in the morning while I made coffee. My mood, my outlook on life, my thoughts and actions began to change. I began to feel better in my spirit and creatively, I blossomed. I knew I was back on the right path. On a whim, I began to post my thoughts of the day online and to my surprise, other people responded favorably. They shared their own stories, their own wisdom. They laughed and cried with me. They supported and encouraged me to complete this book. So, as much as this book is dedicated to the women in my life who have nurtured and taught me and filled me with life lessons, it is also for my online friends who follow me, reading every post, and whose support made this project possible.

To my friends who have chosen to be by my side on this journey of life, I love you more than you know. And to all of my nieces and nephews, you are the true loves of my life.

The intention of this book is to make you think and sometimes make you laugh. I want you to reminisce about the wisdom in your own life and where it comes from. Ultimately though, I want to inspire you to do the things that you love and follow your passions and dreams for you are literally holding my dream come true.

Cultivate Your Own Style

When I was 13, my mother allowed me to go to the mall without her for the first time. My cousin needed to shop for school clothes so this was a perfect opportunity for me to tag along and feel grown up. As a lifelong Catholic school girl, I never experienced the late summer ritual of shopping for new school clothes so this was exciting. My mother gave me $80 to spend, more money than I'd ever had at once. More important than the money, and what has proven to be far more valuable, was the advice she gave me before I left home:

Just because they sell it in your size don't mean you have to buy it.

My mother wanted me to know that I didn't have to spend my money on anything trendy or anything that my friends had or anything that a sales clerk said I should have. She wanted me to figure out what worked for me. Just because the store carried my size, didn't mean it worked for ME. That advice freed me. It freed me to never feel like I wasn't good enough because I wasn't wearing the same clothes as the "in" crowd. To this day, I wear what makes me feel comfortable and what makes me feel good.

This advice has carried over into my business life as well. I stay in my own lane. I don't have to continually change myself or my aesthetic to match other people's style. I trust my own. I trust my design eye. I trust my opinion. So, I am comfortable knowing what the trends are while feeling no obligation to follow them.

In the end, knowing your style is more than just selecting an outfit. It is, instead, getting to the core of who you are and being comfortable in your own skin.

Everyone Creates Their Own Truth

Everyone's truth is filtered through the lens of their own experiences. When we accept that fact, we are free to seek common ground. If a person enters a discussion with the sole purpose of being right, then what happens is not a conversation but a battle. Battles don't end in peace or compromise. They end in carnage.

Accepting that there are always multiple versions of the truth allows us to decide the points on which we agree. The points of agreement become the facts. Based upon those facts, it becomes possible to move to common ground on the remainder of the points or at the very least, move to mutual understanding.

I may not agree with where you are but I understand how you got there.

If people can understand each other's journey and have compassion for that journey, then it's infinitely more difficult to dismiss them as just being wrong or just being liars because their truth doesn't jive with your own.

We all bring our history to the table. Another person's truth is the sum total of their life experiences. We cannot devalue it simply because we didn't live it.

Speak the Truth or Don't Speak

When I was a kid, I saw the great teacher Maya Angelou on the Oprah Winfrey Show. She said, and I'm totally paraphrasing according to my memory of the moment, that "You don't have to say anything, but if you choose to, say the truth." This kernel of wisdom blew my mind because it was the first time I truly realized speaking is a choice. I was always taught to speak when spoken to; when asked a question, to answer. I was taught how to speak publically and in private conversations amongst friends. Speaking came naturally What took a much longer time to learn, however, was knowing when to shut up.

Anything unkind, untrue, unbelievable or plain ridiculous can come out if you talk constantly without a filter. It's easy to feel obligated to be on stage. Being the center of attention is addictive. But, what does it do to your soul to have to say more outrageous things to keep people interested?

Sometimes it's better to just shut up.

You don't have to say anything. Nothing. Silence really is golden. Authenticity is developed through trust. It's important for the world to know that when your mouth is open, true words are coming out.

I'm not perfect. I sometimes hear myself saying things that give me pause upon reflection. But for the most part, I have developed an internal meter which constantly asks: what is my intention? What is the point and purpose of this conversation? Am I trying to uplift or destroy? It forces me to own all of my words both good and bad because the bottom line is that the choice to speak is always mine.

Make
BIG
Plans

During my first semester of graduate school studying Urban Planning, I fell in love with Daniel Burnham. Burnham was an American architect whose work was influential in creating the Chicago skyline. One of the things I admired about him was that he was fond of saying: "Make no little plans for they have no magic to stir men's blood." What he was saying then and continues to teach us is that we must always plan big. Plan huge.

Plan big enough to get excited and a little scared.

Make a plan so big that we have no idea what it truly looks like when it's done and no idea how to get there but our souls can't rest until we figure out how to give this plan life. This process is the essence of creativity. This is the process of genius. Dream an outrageous dream. Make it happen.

Don't Practice the Wrong Technique

There are many wonderful words of wisdom encouraging people to never stay down when they are down, to get up, and to get back in the game. For the most part, they are all right. Yes, get back up, get back in the game. But I add one critical caveat: figure out why you're falling in the first place.

If a wide receiver in football continuously drops the ball, the response will not be to just keep throwing to him. Instead, the coaching staff will sit with the athlete, review game footage, look at every minute movement he makes when attempting to catch the ball and figure out why he's dropping it in the first place. It's ridiculous to continue to do the same thing that's getting you back to the same place you don't want to be with no analysis of how you got there.

Take a step back

Perhaps this athlete is making too many steps. Perhaps he isn't extending his arms far enough. He could be anticipating the ball and moving too soon or not cradling the ball properly once it is caught causing him to drop it. Regardless, it takes careful evaluation to figure out the problem and then practice his way out of it. Stop practicing the wrong technique. Why continue to fall and never know why? The difference between falling six times and not seven may be a simple tweak in strategy. *A tiny adjustment could mean the difference between constant falling and constant success.* In the case of my pro-athlete, figuring out why he drops the ball and practicing good technique could one day result in holding the Lombardi championship trophy with his teammates instead of spending a long off-season wondering what went wrong.

Know Better.
Do Better.
Repeat.

I had a long chat with a friend who is going through a new life growing phase. Our chat included topics like self-esteem and self-worth, trusting your instincts and standing in the truth of yourself. The topic that struck me most was regret.

For the most part, I have no regrets. Well I do regret not buying a piece of art I fell in love with years ago. Other than that, I don't harbor regrets. And for that, I have to thank two people: Maya Angelou and Oprah Winfrey. As a young girl who raced home every day to watch The Oprah Winfrey Show, I was introduced to the majesty of Maya and began reading all her books. In *I Know Why the Caged Bird Sings*, Maya writes the phrase, "When you know better, you do better." Oprah repeated this phrase hundreds of times over the years but it didn't sink in to my heart until I was 23 years old.

From age 15 on, I wrote in journals every day. Then on my birthday each year, I would read the previous year's entries which inevitably ended with me crying at how stupid I thought I was based on decisions I'd made in the past. On my 23rd birthday, I'd had enough. I realized that every decision I make today could be proven wrong with 365 days of hindsight. Therefore, I would make the best decisions I could with the information I had and when I knew better, I would do better.

Fully internalizing that thought into my heart changed my life. I don't regret any decisions. I know I did the best I could. And even when I didn't do my best, I can make another choice. Do better when you know better. The words are simple but so profound. They freed me from harboring negative feelings about my past. They freed me from second-guessing myself. For that, I am grateful.

Just let it all go. Trust your instincts. Take the best info you have and make the best decision you can and move on because when you know better, you can do better.

What Brings You Joy?

Have you ever considered what brings you joy? We hear talk all the time about striving to be happy. But, do we ever consider the difference between what brings happiness and what brings joy?

One of my first lessons on the difference came while watching The Oprah Show when the guest was none other than Arnold Schwarzenegger. He told Oprah about a conversation he had with then wife, Maria Shriver. He said that he told Maria to not count on him to make her happy. The audience immediately groaned and booed but Oprah asked them to let him continue his point. He explained further that what makes you happy changes. He's 100% right. What made you happy as a child isn't what makes you happy as a teen or an adult. The tv show that made you happy last season bores you to tears this season. The pair of jeans you used to be happy to wear now seems out of date and you never touch them. Therefore, it isn't fair to put the burden of your happiness onto another person. Other people can support our happiness. They can facilitate our happiness. But they can't be the thing that makes us happy. When your child sings "London Bridge is falling down…" the first five times, it may make you happy. By the 100th time, you want to tear your ears off! People change. They have to live their own lives and their own truth. It's not their responsibility to make us happy.

Joy comes from the intangibles. We may not derive happiness from hearing our kids sing the same tune over and over again, but knowing that our kids love to sing brings us joy. Even stationery, which brings me immense joy, has parts of the creation process that don't make me happy anymore. Try cutting 100 yards of ribbon into eleven inch strips and see how long it takes for that job to become tedious and nothing close to resembling happiness. However, the fact that I get to create stationery brings me joy so I tolerate the parts that don't make me happy.

True joy is deep, underlying, and soul-stirring. Happiness can be fleeting. Joy resonates. Joy lasts. Focus on what brings you joy and the little annoyances along the way won't matter.

NOW is the new January

We all have changes in our lives that we want to make, that we know we should make. We decide it would be a really good New Year's resolution. By the time January rolls around, we've either forgotten or get excited and fizzle out by mid-February. There's too much pressure on January. We can all decide that now, whatever month it is, is as good a time as any to begin. Now is the best time because it's the only time we can control.

What is your NOW resolution? What can you get accomplished by January if you started today? What's your big dream, your audacious goal? Work together with a friend or partner. Find someone to hold you accountable and who will encourage you to succeed. There is no need to wait until the New Year to start a life revolution. NOW is the new January.

Savor the Good Memories

On The Tonight Show, Jimmy Fallon asked Senator Cory Booker about his college football playing days. Cory's response: "The older I get; the better I was!" Everybody started laughing and even Heidi Klum told him she'd have to remember that line. Why? Because it's awesome and awesomely funny and SO TRUE!

Once you cross a certain threshold in life, the past becomes malleable. You can make it whatever you want. If you were an average sportsman in high school, forever you re-tell that story as if you were one shot away from greatness. It's fun. The older I get the better dancer I was in my youth. Oh, I was a master on the dance floor! (Sure I was!)

Eventually life evens out. Eventually you fall into the pocket of who you were meant to be. Your friends are real. Your family chills out. Your work is what it is. And your past is the past. You forget about all the bad stuff and take joy in reminiscing about the good old days. And "remember that time" stories with your friends get bigger and the tales taller. Life is fun. The older you get, the better you can create the present but also the better you can recreate the past.

Self-doubt is not a Friend

With a lot of creative endeavors in action right now, I should be pretty happy. I like all of the projects I'm working on. I like the clients I'm working with. Also, I'm collaborating with an old and dear friend who is also a fellow designer. If I kept a physical, written Life Agenda (which perhaps I should consider doing), I could pretty much move "Live my dreams" to the done column. I could do all of that if self-doubt didn't insist upon visiting me every day and grossly overstaying its welcome.

I believe in self-evaluation and introspection. I do it perhaps more than I should. I like the self-check of reminding myself to live with the intentions of my heart. But, self-doubt doesn't bring enlightenment or a new perspective or creativity. Self-doubt is a slippery slope to fear. Fear leads to inaction or worse, decision-making based on flawed thoughts.

Self-doubt creeps slyly. It says, "I just want you to be sure this is right." Then it slowly builds to: "are YOU right? Are YOU the best person to do this? Can YOU accomplish this?"

Last night, I was working on a new line of cards for the shop. I knew exactly what I wanted them to be, exactly the direction I wanted to go, exactly how I wanted them to look. But as soon as I opened the laptop and began to work, self-doubt paralyzed me. I got nothing done because I questioned every move, every line. I became so frustrated that I quit working for the night.

Perhaps a good night's sleep is what I needed because today, I am looking my self-doubt squarely in the eye and kicking it out of my mind. I trust my instincts, my talent, and my creative abilities. If the world loves what I create, that's wonderful. I mean, the ultimate goal is to sell stationery. Regardless, I will know that I didn't doubt my vision or myself and I followed through on what I wanted to create. **Self-doubt is not my friend and it isn't yours either.**

Calm Down

Most days, I feel like I'm operating at a consistent level eight. If that were really true, surely I'd get more tasks accomplished. The cold dose of truth is that I stress myself out so much over what I should do that it paralyzes me from actually doing anything. Stress makes me feel like my activity level is at eight, sometimes nine, occasionally ten when the actual work is consistently between four and six. So, my goal is to calm down. Calm way down. Cut myself some slack. Chill out. Make a plan. Follow it. No more. No less. No longer will I syphon my energy away from the things I really desire to achieve by stressing over details I cannot control. Stress prevents me from appreciating what I have, who I am, how far I've come, and what I have accomplished. Stress, therefore, has got to go.

Calm down.

Chill out.

Breathe.

Today is a
Good Day
No Matter
What

It has taken me a long time to fully understand that every day is good. Let that sink in. Every day is good. In any day, bad things can happen. But every day we're alive is a good day. Every day that we get another chance to make better choices, laugh with our friends, see the sun rise and set, do what we love, be with whom we love, and be fully ourselves, is a good day. There can be unpleasant events or downright, devastatingly awful things that rip apart our hearts. But, if we can go to bed at night having survived, it's a good day. The day equals life. Life holds infinite possibility of growth. Life can always change. And life, in every day it brings us, is good.

Be Yourself

Often it is said that imitation is the sincerest form of flattery. Sometimes though, imitation is the easiest cop out. If you're busy imitating someone else, then you don't have to invest any time in cultivating yourself. It's harder to recognize, appreciate, practice, and most of all, enjoy your own talent. **Appreciate your own idiosyncrasies, your own quirks, your own little ways of operating or thinking.** That quirk may be just the one thing that someone else absolutely loves about you.

Bake a New Cake

There will always be times when things don't go our way. It can range from a minor inconvenience to a major catastrophe. During these times, we lose our equilibrium. We don't know what to do or where to turn. All we want is a crumb of the familiar, a sweet taste of what we already know. **Many of us spend years picking at the crumbs of the past never realizing that we have all the ingredients to bake a new cake.**

Life happens. We lose jobs, get divorced, and fail at desperately desired goals. Far too often, we act as if these events remove irretrievable parts of ourselves. So, we settle. We settle for crumbs. It's easy to long for what we used to have. Jobs provide security. Relationships provide comfort. It's easy to fool ourselves into believing that no cake will ever taste as decadent as the one we just had. What I know to be true and what Hurricane Katrina taught me for sure, is that outside events take nothing away from who we are inside. We retain all the ingredients inside of us to make magic happen. Bake a new cake. Life doesn't steal our ingredients. All of them are still there waiting for us to light a fire in our ovens and start mixing. The beauty of life is that wisdom makes us better bakers. We can take what we've been through and use that wisdom to craft a better recipe, a more flavorful cake. Don't settle for crumbs when you have the capacity to create a masterpiece!

Be Overwhelmed by Gratitude

I received a complimentary email from a customer who loved her stationery and it was so nice that I couldn't fully receive it. Sometimes receiving the weight of someone else's gratitude feels self-aggrandizing. Haven't we all been taught that it's best to be humble? In the face of someone giving us a sincere thanks, isn't giving a kind nod and humble "you're welcome" all we're supposed to do?

Well I want to celebrate. And I want to be overwhelmed with the joy that's being given back to me. It's so easy for us to think of karma in a negative light but we don't want to receive it when it comes back as goodness and love. Be overwhelmed by the love you receive, by the kindness, by the well wishes. They are a direct result of what you've put out into the world. I say all the time, "I hope you love these cards as much as I do." I am overwhelmed when they actually do! I feel like Sally Field, "You like me! You really like me!" Allow yourself to be overwhelmed by the good in life. Feel it so deeply that it moves you to tears or to dance or to sing in joy. There is nothing wrong in believing a compliment. There's nothing wrong in being so in the moment of gratitude when you know you've done your best to stand back and let the waves of applause energize your body and soul. Be mindful of what you put out in the world and be grateful when that goodness comes back.

Write More.
Text Less.

On a daily basis, I hear folks waxing poetically about the beauty of stationery and how awesome it is to receive handwritten notes. They also lament how sad it is that said notes are not as common as they used to be. On the opposite pole, I hear an equal amount of people saying they don't send notes because their handwriting is poor. My response is always the same: "Who cares?" No one cares if your penmanship is poor. They only care that you cared enough to send them a note. And yes, it may take a minute longer to read it. So what? No one will ever say, "Stop sending me notes until you practice your penmanship." Your handwriting is your personal expression. If you want to write in perfect Spencerian or Palmer's penmanship, then you can practice it. Most of us don't. And it's okay.

There's nothing like holding a piece of paper in your hands and knowing that someone took the time to put pen to paper and write these words just for you. I keep all of the notes I receive in a box on my desk and every time I feel low, need a pick me up, or just need a laugh, I reread some of them and they lift my spirits.

Texting is great. It's an effective, quick form of communication that is going nowhere. It's essential to modern life. I text all the time. But, there has to be a balance. There has to be a moment when you slow down, consider each word, consider the person you're writing to, consider the paper you're writing on, consider the pen, and carefully orchestrate a moment when your loved one opens the envelope and read how you feel.

I Think I Can

Lately I've had several conversations with my friends about life transformations. We're entering our forties and although everyone isn't at the same station in life, most are asking the same questions: How is the second act of my life going to be different from the first? Am I going to do better because I know better?

I can talk a good game. But I had to ask myself if my own actions were backing up my words. The resistance I'm feeling is coming from areas of inauthenticity. There are areas of my life where I say I want change but my inaction says loud and clear that I don't or that I'm not ready or that I don't believe enough yet. So I've decided to heed the advice given years ago by The Little Engine that Could. I'm going to baby step on faith in the areas that scare me and leap in the areas I'm confident. But I will not remain stagnant. The second act of my life is about to be awesome because I think I can… I think I can… I think I can… Now GO!

Think the Next Thought

When I finished grad school, I accepted a job in the Mayor's Office of Economic Development where I met and worked with a woman who would become one of my greatest mentors, Gwen Boutté Owens. Many of the things she taught me in our far too brief time together, I carry with me. The first and greatest of these is, think the next thought.

When I first started, I brought every problem to her no matter how small. One day, I walked in her office to lay out the current situation. She listened intently and then calmly asked, "Did you think the next thought?" She continued to ask me what would I do, what I thought she would do, what was the best course of action based on the knowledge I had of all the moving parts. When I explained all that, she said, "Okay, fix it."

What I realized in that moment was that my job was not to bring her problems. My job was to bring her solutions. She didn't need me to feed her ego by making her think she had all the answers. She was far more interested in developing my talent and my instincts. A few years later, breast cancer took my Gwen away. To this day, when I feel myself becoming overwhelmed by an issue, I tell myself to think the next thought. What's next? What are the options? What are the best solutions? It's easy to get caught up in problems. It's more useful to get caught up in solutions.

Celebrate Your Opposites

One of my best friends asked me to create a custom design for her. Sure, not a problem, anything for a friend. I asked her, "What style do you want?" And she responded, "Anything you think is really cool and would be totally great for you, do the complete opposite!" We laughed for fifteen minutes after that because I KNEW that's what she would say. We laughed because we have known since the infancy of our friendship over ten years ago that our personal styles, what we naturally gravitate towards, are polar opposites. This doesn't mean we don't ever like the same thing, we often do. But seven times out of ten, it's not even close. And that is beautiful.

The people around you should challenge your comfort zone. They should enable you to see the world in a different way, to expand your thinking. If everyone in your life believes and thinks and acts the exact same way you do, I hate to be the one to inform you, but you are in a cult. Seek help immediately. Seriously though, my friend comes alive in a sea of bright color and is as obsessive about tie-dye as I am monochromatic minimalism. According to her, I've never seen a shade of grey I didn't fall in love with (and no, that's not a literature reference for it was intended literally). And she's right.

I love the fact that my friends have varied interests. They help me discover new things. They expand my mind. And ultimately, they are a constant reminder that people can have divergent beliefs and still love and respect one another.

Forgive Before the Fight

This morning I caught myself about to unleash a beast. This beast is ferocious and cunning and will commit random acts of ridiculousness unbeknownst to mankind. This beast often manifests first as the thought, "I wish you would."

Let me explain. I started thinking about an issue that would/could potentially cause a rift between myself and another person. I then began to say, "Oh I wish they would bring that up because then I'd say this, then that, followed by…" on and on and on. Next thing I know; I'm preparing for a battle that isn't even remotely about to happen. If I had let that emotion fester, then I'd spend my days waiting for the spark to commence the battle I created (inside my own mind) can begin and the other person would have no idea what they have come up against.

And I thought, "This is stupid." So I stopped and asked myself if my relationship was bigger than the subject of that fight. Did it mean more to me? Was the perceived transgression something I would/could forgive? Yes? Then forgive before the fight and move on. **Don't create negativity with people based on one random negative thought on one random morning.** Oh and one thing I forgot, getting into arguments post forty is ridiculous in and of itself. By now, conflict resolution should have been learned. So beast, go back to bed. Your services are not needed here.

Get a Hobby

This morning I looked up in my office and saw a painting I did over ten years ago. I never had a desire to be a painter. I saw my friends in college who had real ability, thought I couldn't possibly do that, and never did. But one day, an ordinary dinner in a restaurant with my then 12-year-old nephew changed everything. He looked at the art behind him and declared to me that he could paint that if he wanted to. Seeing this as a teaching moment, I asked, "If I got you the materials would you paint it for me?" He said yes and I was off to the races. I bought every canvas, brush, paint, and accessory I could think of because I thought; finally, I've found this kid's passion. Needless to say, he never touched any of it.

I was so disappointed but decided to try it myself and I loved it! It doesn't matter that I'm not the best painter, what matters is that I can get lost in the creation process and then hang the fruit of that labor on my wall. I became obsessed with painting all the time. Painting convinced me that we all need a hobby. We need something that removes us from our routines and shifts our focus. Stress kills and we are all mired under it. Find something you'd like to do that creates beauty. My friends might say I have too many hobbies, but I truly love tackling new craft projects and working with my hands. There are so many things in the world that we have to do, should do, and must do. It's imperative that we spend some time doing what we want to do.

Your Voice Has Value

When I was a sophomore in high school, a class discussion turned pretty racist and had me so angry I couldn't wait to get home to tell my mother. Today, I don't remember the details of the discussion. But I do remember the conversation with my mama. When I arrived home, she was doing dishes. I unloaded on her about who said what and then so-and-so said this then that. She stopped me mid rant without ever turning from the dishes and asked, "And what did YOU say?" I told her that I didn't say anything and continued ranting. She says, "Stop. I don't want to hear your story." I was shocked and yelled, "But it was RACIST!!" She calmly replied, "And you did NOTHING. I pay the same amount of tuition as the other girls' parents. Your voice costs the same as theirs. So if you can't use it when you're supposed to, don't use it with me now."

At first, I was mad at her because she wouldn't listen to me. Then, I was mad at myself because she was right. Of all the lessons, I've learned from my mother, this one has followed my journey most closely. I don't believe in not talking to people about race, politics, or religion. I believe that if you bring compassion for another's point of view then you can talk to anyone about anything. But you have to know intrinsically that there is value in your voice and in your experience and in theirs. I assure you anyone who has been in a classroom or board room with me since that day with my mother can attest that I know the value of my voice. I'm not afraid to speak when I feel something is wrong and I'm equally as willing to give credit when it's due.

Speak up! There may be other people who agree with you don't have the courage to speak. Speak up for the people who opened doors for you. Speak up for those whose voices will never be heard. At the end of the day, you have to decide that the courage to enlighten far outweighs the desire to not offend. Sometimes people need to be offended. Sometimes they need to be confronted with a different truth. It's okay. Silencing yourself does nothing. Having the confidence to use your voice to stand for your principles can change the world. My voice has value and yours does too.

Don't do Wrong Just Because it's Fun

There's an iPad app called Addicus that my two-year-old niece loves. I thought it would be a great teaching tool to move from number recognition to addition. And it would be, if she played it correctly. The game has a critical design flaw. When you get the right answer, nothing happens. But when you click the wrong answer, it makes a huge popping sound and all the little number mushrooms explode. The 2 year old loves it. So even though she KNOWS the right answer, she presses the wrong one to get the reward and screams, "Oopsy Daisy! POP!!" Now that's cute when you're two, but we have a lot of adult people doing the wrong things and making crazy decisions just because the reward is more fun than doing the right thing. Right isn't always fun. Right isn't always easy. But right plays to a long game. The easy wrong feels good now and only leads to a long game of regret. Let me say that doing wrong isn't always illegal or immoral, it could be as simple as not being honest with yourself, making promises and not keeping them. It's all the little things we do to keep the hard tasks at bay just a little while longer. There's a difference between making an honest mistake and intentionally making the wrong choice. **Be careful of doing wrong because it feels good now as later will tell a much different story.**

The Thought Never Counts More than the Action

We have all heard or said "it's the thought that counts." I have many times but have never considered the real meaning until now. The thought alone never counts. Consider this: husband comes to his wife on their anniversary. He says, "My love, I have been thinking for weeks about the perfect gift for you: jewels, a vacation, a spa day. I've thought about everything." Then he walks away. The wife says, "Well what did you get?" He says, "Nothing. I THOUGHT about it." Do you remotely think she will say "Oh well, it's the thought that counts?" Heck no! That guy just bought a first class ticket to the dog house. If only thoughts counted, my body would be amazing from all my thoughts about being a beast in the gym. If the thoughts counted, I would only eat food I grew myself using my own compost and salvaged rain water. Nobody calls you a thoughtful person because of your thoughts alone. They say it when you act. "Thanks for thinking of me" literally means "Thanks for thinking of me AND taking the time to DO this nice thing you did for me." We don't write "To think" lists. We write "To DO" lists because the action makes the thoughts real. This is why the quality of our thoughts are so important. What we think about, we manifest. The action always counts more than the thoughts. Even the people who are lauded as great thinkers are only lauded because they performed the action of preserving those thoughts on a tangible medium be it books, or film, or recordings.

These thoughts of the day were nothing until I started to write and share them. I used to think about these things alone over my morning coffee. Now I have interesting conversations with people every day. The act of posting them made it real. And I'm so grateful for all of the people who take the time to read them and write to me. Your actions make my entire day!

Yes, you know. But Do You Understand?

How many times have you ever had a conversation with someone, thought you were communicating the same thing, but in the end the two of you are baffled as to how you could have interpreted each other's wishes so wrong? I call this: "We're on the same page but we're reading totally different books!" Learning to communicate effectively is critical to getting what you want in life. Nowadays, people are quick to rush through everything and not fully engage so meanings are lost in translation. It takes more time to fix a misunderstanding than it does to make sure the understanding is correct in the first place. Slow down. Listen. Ask questions. Be sure that you mean the same thing even when saying the same words. My friend and I can both say we like "bold color." When I say it, I mean a pop of color on a ground of grey. When my friend says "bold color," she means a cornucopia of bright color sliding down a rainbow. Same page. Different book. Next time you're having a conversation, ask the questions that get to the true heart of the issue because "I know what you're saying" is far different from "I understand what you mean."

It's Okay to
Have a Fit
for a
Little Bit

When things beyond my control have gone awry but were my responsibility to fix, I cannot tell you I have always responded with a calm but determined demeanor. I've been known to say to my friends and colleagues, "Give me 15 minutes to freak out and I'll be ready." I need 15 minutes to curse or cry or let out frustration and just have a plain old fit in private to get out of the negative energy I'm feeling. Then I can move forward and get the job done. The older I've gotten, my 15 minutes have become more theoretical. In practice, I need about seven minutes. Whatever your time is, it's okay. It's okay to have a full on fit if you need to just to exorcise the energy that's going to hold you back from thinking clearly. You can't make good decisions when you're pissed off. If your mind is focused on being angry at the problem or the situation or the person, then you cannot think clearly enough to truly look at it objectively. Once you've let the negative energy out, let it stay gone. And do not take your frustrations out on other people; that's counterproductive. Find an alone place: close the door: curse like a sailor: move on. It's better to take 15 minutes to compose yourself and get your mind right than to compound the problem because you were too angry to think straight.

You Have to Impress No One

A lot of my acquaintances are interior designers and as such I am privy to their conversations, inspirations, and trends. I love it. I love talking about how changing a sofa or adding a subtle hint of gold can change the whole look and feel of a room. I see blogs every day and some of the bloggers' homes seem preternaturally perfect at all times. Their kids are never messy except in a cute way with great lighting of course. All of this is great, for them. I had a conversation with two random dads this morning about their kids and their homes and about how, try as they might; it's never clean enough, never finished enough, never perfect. It's real life. **Most everyday people are just making do with what they have. It's okay to aspire to have better things. It's not okay to feel horrible about what you have and about how you live because it seems someone else lives better.** Curate your own home. Cultivate your own version of the good life. Of course, you can borrow ideas from bloggers and magazines and movies. But, don't get caught up in trying to impress everyone or anyone or keep up with the Joneses (or the Kardashians) because you never know what's really going on at their house anyway.

Actions
Never Leave
Home
Without
Consequences

One of the strangest things in the world to me is the crazy phenomena which leads people to believe their actions not only do not, but should not have consequences. There is someone in my life that has no filter. For as long as I can remember, they have had a tendency to just say whatever is on their mind without regard to the truth, experience, or feelings of the other person or anyone else in the room. Then they get angry when anyone calls them out on it. It's as if they believe their actions, their freedom to speak, are paramount over everyone else's right to react.

You can say whatever mean thing you want. But you don't get to be surprised when other people respond to you in a manner equal to your ferocity. You don't get to act and then demand no consequences. If you don't want a speeding ticket, don't speed. If you don't want a room full of people to treat you poorly, don't walk in being rude to them. If you want to win the game, show up to practice. If you want to win at life, show up and participate. Do you. Do whatever it is you want. Just know that whatever action you choose is also the consequence you choose.

Say "I Love You"

Last week, I decided to write notes to everyone who had been on my mind or to whom I owed a delinquent thank you. What I got back in terms of gratitude and people's stories far outweighed my expectations. So many people said to me, "I needed your words today." That led me to thinking, "Is there ever a time when we don't NEED to hear we're special or that someone cares?" No. If your loved one says, "I love you," you don't follow it up with, "Thanks but I didn't need to hear that today. Can you save it for a day when I do?" We need it every day, any day. It's always a good day. Let someone know they're special and appreciated. The best day is today and the only time is now.

Credit is Not Necessary

You know that person, the one who never misses an opportunity to announce what they did? They're the one who brings food to a sick friend and then talk about it every chance they get to anyone who will listen. They're the one who you beg to not do anything because you KNOW you'll hear about it forever. Yes, that one. That person drives me nuts. I believe that if you are genuinely a kind and caring person, then it shouldn't matter if you never get any credit. If someone is at a low point and you help them, they don't need to be reminded of it and made to feel forever beholden to you. And you don't have the right to prostitute someone else's story just to make yourself look good. There have been times in my life when people have helped me in deep, meaningful ways and they've never wanted an ounce of credit. I have one friend from high school whose act of kindness was so profound to me but so second nature to her that she always seems embarrassed when I bring it up. On the other hand, I was recently in a situation where someone volunteered themselves unasked and did a favor for a friend of mine. They then proceeded to talk about it incessantly forcing my friend to publicly thank them over and over. It was a grotesque display of narcissism and I was appalled. If you're going to be nice, do it even if nobody will ever know. Do it especially if nobody will ever know. Karma will bring you exactly what you deserve.

You're Awesome. Believe it.

One day, I was scribbling aimlessly in a notebook. When I actually paid attention to what I'd written, it read "How many times do you have to prove that you're awesome before you believe it?" I was quite shocked but it also made me take a step back and evaluate. There are so many things in life I wish were different. There are many paths I should have taken. If I decided to stay in that energy space, I could easily fall into a depression supported by all the what ifs I could muster. But, I decided to read my own words, cut myself some slack and review the litany of things I've done that make me a pretty awesome woman. I'm not perfect but I'm proud of how I treat people. I'm proud that I followed my stationery dreams when nearly every person in my life at the time, except my then 5-year-old niece thought I was crazy. I'm proud of the motley crew of friends I've met along the way who accept and love me even when I don't come to their birthday parties or baby showers! Concentrate on what makes you awesome! Make a list. Read it over and over. You've already proven it, now it's time to believe it.

Boredom is a Choice

I learned early to never to tell my mother I was bored. Her response was always the same: "Then you're a boring person." I didn't care for that remark at all. My mother says to this day, "There are no boring times, just boring people"

She believes that the world is too big, too vast, that there's always something to do. Go somewhere you've never been, read a book, listen to good music. There's just way too much happening to ever be bored. If you can't find anything amusing or exciting, then you must be a boring person.

The cure is to develop a natural curiosity for learning and exploring. There are always new experiences waiting to be discovered.

Once in high school, I told my mother I was bored. She made my cousin and me go to a cereal manufacturers' trade show she read about in the newspaper. To this day, it's one of the coolest (and still ridiculous) experiences I've ever had. And to my ultimate surprise, I ended up winning a year's supply of cereal (which they gave me in three industrial sized garbage bags I had to lug home)! I thank her for teaching me that boredom is a choice. Choose to be excited and interested about things and eventually that's how the world will describe you. By the way, my mother made me walk my neighborhood and give most of that cereal away. Boredom cured forever!

Cultivate Curiosity

If boredom is a choice, then the opposite choice naturally, has to be curiosity. Cultivate a natural curiosity for the world around. If you like a flower, for example, do a little research about it. Read what it needs to grow, its soil requirements, where it originates from, if it's a hybrid, etc. Learn everything you can. Learning about things in depth moves the needle from appreciation to respect. The same goes for people. If you take the time to learn someone's story, then you can move from being acquaintances to being friends. It's easy to want to stay in your own bubble and never venture out.

Developing a curiosity about our world makes you want to see it up close. Curiosity makes you an adventurer. It gives you a safe space to dream.

What if learning about those flowers inspires you to open a nursery to teach others why they should learn about and appreciate these flowers? You never know where the journey will lead. How would I have ever known that walking into a chain paper store when I was in 8th grade would put me on a stationery path that led me here? Be curious! You may discover a passion that will change your life.

Cherish
Old Friends

Last night, Eddie Murphy was on the Arsenio Hall Show. I had to watch as the reclusive Murphy is one of my favorite comedians of all time. And I knew, for as private as he is, he would come out of his shell around long-time best friend Arsenio. The interview did not disappoint. The best part was recognizing my relationships with my old friends in their rapport with each other. Old friendships are the ones in which you don't even have to tell the whole story. All you say is "Remember that time …" and you both laugh for an hour and no one else knows what's going on.

Old friends are the keepers of your secrets, the markers of your history. They know the truth of who you are and the circumstances that made you that way.

They overlook your shortcomings and praise your achievements. They want nothing but the best for you. They are the first to laugh at you and the first to defend you. I'm so blessed to have a number of women about whom I could literally cry right now because their friendship and loyalty and laughs mean so much to me. The story of my life is incomplete without them. Reach out to your old friends. Keep that flame lit because one day, when age has removed the details, it will be beautiful to look into the eyes of an old friend, say "Remember that time…" and smile because they do.

Don't Bury Your Dreams

My mother is on the bereavement committee at church so whenever someone passes away, there's a phone call and a long discussion about the person's life and arrangements and protocols of Catholic burials and lots of "I'm sorry for your loss." When one of these conversations is going on, I find myself wondering if the deceased lived their dreams. Did they follow their passion and see it through or is this another unrealized dream littering the graveyard? Give life to your dreams. It's been said that there's nothing sadder than wasted potential. Don't waste yours. What I learned in creating Write Robinson is that I had a right to live my dreams just as much as the next person. And so do you. We all have the right to at least try. If it doesn't work out, you can choose to leave it alone or learn from why it didn't work and try again. At least you did something. And who cares if it doesn't work? It's okay. It's all good. Worst case scenario is that for the rest of your life, you'll have a story to tell about that time you threw caution to the wind and dared to be awesome. Holding your dreams inside doesn't serve you or the world. When I go, I want the world to know I gave my dreams my best shot.

Complaining is not a Strategy

We all know someone who, when faced with either a major obstacle or a minor inconvenience, will complain with equal vigor and intensity. No accommodation will suffice. Nothing ever fixes their problem. Then somehow, some way, when nothing gets accomplished, it's everyone's fault but their own. They are addicted to complaining. They have not learned that complaining is not a strategy. It's okay to freak out for a minute, to get all the negative feelings out first and then start fixing the problem. Chronic complainers never get to the fixing phase because they get stuck in the drama of the perceived transgression. Complaining is not a plan, not a course of action, not a strategy. Complaining can bring awareness to an injustice, but it does not communicate a solution. When I was in college, I worked in the campus dining hall and part of my job was to read comment cards to relay to the cooking staff. I cannot tell you how many times I had to explain that "This food sucks" was not constructive. The complaint did nothing and was a waste of my time and the author's. Instead had she written, "The sauce is too salty," I could have solved this problem. Complaints are nothing if they don't provide a roadmap to the solution. Complaining that your city's streets are horrible does nothing. A list of specific potholes in your neighborhood accompanied by a petition of homeowners will get noticed. So while complaining might feel good in the moment because you're letting off steam, long-term chronic complaining just makes you a bitter person. You can no longer see the good in the world because nothing is ever perfect enough. Complaining is not a strategy.

Save Yourself

While playing with blocks with my two-year-old niece, I had a chat with her that she'll never remember but I hope somewhere inside of her, it's stored for later. Every time we'd stack the blocks, she'd say, "We built a castle!" Then I'd respond, "That's right! Build your own castle!" As I looked at this gorgeous child, I needed to tell her that she doesn't have to ever wait for a prince to come to start living her life. No prince has to save her. She can save herself. If she wants a castle, she can build it herself. She has the right and the talent and the intellect to create the life she wants and then, if she so chooses, she can find a suitable prince to be her partner in life. So many women I know have the "Someday my prince will come" mentality. They believe that life will not truly begin until a glass slipper is placed on their foot and they are whisked away to happily ever after. That is a fallacy. Live your life. Be who you are. Develop your own sensibilities, culture, tastes. Become an interesting person! If you do nothing but wait on the prince, what will he find when he arrives? What do you bring to the table? Save yourself. Buy your own glass slipper if that's the kind of shoe you like. Send yourself flowers. Treat yourself the way you want to be treated by your partner. Enjoy your living. Build your own castle. Then, when you choose to become someone's princess, you come as a whole woman needing a whole man, not as a little girl waiting for someone to turn on the light switch of her life.

Fail Sometimes

Alone making stationery gave me a lot of time to think last night and for some reason I had a good long laugh at the many things I've tried and failed over the years. There are some minor things, some major. But the common thread is that I've failed them all. This is the point where I should probably start talking about trying again and dusting yourself off to get back in the game. The truth is, though, I believe there are some things that you just chalk up to a failure and let it be. I'm comfortable with the fact that I'm never going to be a roller-skater. I tried for nearly a year. Every afternoon I laced the fancy skates my grandmother bought me, got my training poles and clumsily rolled up and down my sidewalk. When I tried to bring my "skills" to an actual rink, I fell so hard and so embarrassingly that I crawled to the changing area, put my sneakers back on and cheered on my friends from the sidelines. I was done. I never put those skates on again. Do I feel like a quitter, a failure? No. I failed at learning to be a good skater. I don't want to skate. My grandmother thought I should learn to skate. I'm cool with being a non-skater. I'm also cool with knowing I tried. I tried and I failed. The whole mantra of keep trying at everything gives a false sense that we should be good at everything or that we want to do everything. Let me be clear, if I truly wanted to be a roller-skating prodigy, then of course, I should have kept trying. I should have figured out what I was doing wrong. I should have gotten up and kept skating. But I knew from the beginning that skating was my grandmother's goal, not mine. We are defined equally by our successes and our failures. Sometimes the failure is just a roadblock saying, "This is not the right path for you." Our life's roadmap isn't at all straight. And it doesn't have to be. We have to take twists and turns and have adventures. Failures just mean don't go that way. Try another path. Pick your battles. Carve your own road. I'll never be a roller skating champion. I failed. Oh well. At least I have a really funny memory of that time I tried.

We are the same.
Our experiences
are different.

Yesterday, I watched an interview series with comedians. Because I've loved stand-up comedy since childhood, I was happy to devote an hour of my time listening to comedians talk about the craft of comedy. One line struck me in a deep place: "the human experience translates." Keenan Ivory Wayans was speaking about structuring a joke and how comedians must be specific. He said that if you say, "all mothers…," the audience will think, "Well my mother doesn't do that." But if you say, "MY mother…," then the audience will either think "My mother does that too!" or they will simply laugh at his mother. The goal is to translate the human experience in a way that gets people to include themselves in the joke. That's what makes it funny.

When I see a picture of an elated child holding a new toy, I know what that feels like. I know that joy. I know that experience. So many times we discard people. We assume that because they don't look like us, talk like us, live like us, eat like us, worship like us, that somehow their human experience is different. It's not. All of our love is the same. All of our joy is the same. Our pain is the same. And if we get out of our own heads, prejudices, predispositions, circle of friends, and neighborhoods, we will see it clearly.

The human experience does translate, if we let it. If we open our hearts and see with lens of our souls, we will see the beauty of our common experiences and that our families are just as beautiful and as messed up as everybody else's family. It's hard to see people through the lens of humanity when your first instinct is to put a label on them and cast them aside. It is only by getting rid of the labels and seeing the human being will we ever begin to truly realize that we truly are all the same.

A Zebra is not a Horse

I have a really good friend who has heard my complaints about the same three people for eleven years. Exasperated, she asked me why I get upset when these people exhibited the same behavior ALL the time. I said to her, "My problem is that I keep looking at zebras and expecting them to act like horses." That realization changed my entire perspective. I am guilty as sin of treating people as I wish they would be and not as they are. A zebra may resemble a horse. It may be a distant cousin to the horse on its mama's side. But it is not and never will be a horse. It doesn't want to be tamed. It doesn't want you to pet it or ride it or race it or keep it as your pet. It will never let you do any of those things. You can try forever and you will never turn that zebra into a horse. It never will be. We can't expect people or animals to act against their nature. And as Maya Angelou says, "When people tell you how they really are, believe them." I refuse to spend another iota of time in my life wishing other people were different or that they acted in a way I think they should. I'm done with that. I'm going to let the zebras be zebras and not get upset or take it personally when they show me their truth. All I can do is work on myself and try to become the best version of myself that I can be. Oh but let's be clear, I still complain about the zebras in my life, I'm just not shocked or hurt anymore when they show me who they are. I believe them.

Smile

When I worked downtown, every morning I'd eat breakfast and write in my journal in the same coffee shop. It had floor to ceiling glass windows so I could see the entire vista of the bustling corner. Usually I sat in the window and people-watched while savoring my coffee. One day, I decided to put on my psychology major hat and try an experiment. For ten minutes, I would look at everyone who passed the window as if they'd said something horrible to me or as if I didn't like them. I'd say no words, just make a face. And for ten minutes, everyone gave me back what I gave to them. Some even flipped me the middle finger! Then, for the next ten minutes, I smiled at everyone. And sure enough, everyone smiled back. Some gave me a polite wave, some an enthusiastic "Good morning!" but they all responded in kind to what I gave out. The great part is that as I began to do this small act every day, I began to see the same people and we'd wave at each other like old friends although the only thing we shared was a morning smile. I smile at the world all the time, even when I don't initially feel like it because I want to see smiling faces back at me. I know that you and I are the nuclei of our experiences. Everything begins with us. What we put out returns. So smile and let the world smile back.

Truth
Outweighs
Feelings

We have all been there. Faced with the conundrum of sparing someone's feelings or telling them the truth, we agonize over which way to go. I made the decision long ago to always go with the truth. Thinking that we can protect someone's feelings is a fallacy. We can't control how anyone feels. We can't control how they deal with their feelings. We can't tell them how long a feeling should last. Not one iota of their feelings is within our purview. Therefore, the most loving thing we can do is to give them the truth so at least the feelings they experience are authentic. We can't live an authentic life with inaccurate information and it is unkind to ask another person to do the same. The bigger problem with withholding information to spare a person's feelings is that it gets worse the longer it takes them to find out. Now you have compounded the problem and perhaps lost the trust of a loved one. Learning to deal with feelings and emotions is part of growing up. Don't deny someone the opportunity to have a learning experience because you want to be the hero. Ignorance is not bliss. Being kept ignorant on purpose is cruel. Do you want to walk around thinking everything is fine only to find out that there was something you needed to know and no one said a word? Would your reaction be: "Oh they loved me so much that they hid the truth?" No. You're angry at them and possibly at whatever the information is as well. Or maybe the information pales in comparison to the betrayal. Think about that the next time you need to speak. Feelings ebb and flow. They come and go. The truth remains. Concern yourself with the truth and the feelings will work out themselves.

Keep Moving

I saw an interview with Diana Nyad after her historic swim from Cuba to Florida. She said, "Whatever your other shore is, get there." It struck me deeply because she put a powerful message of perseverance so succinctly.

Just get there. Keep moving.

Get there. Don't quit.

Get there. It will be alright.

Just get there.

We all have oceans to cross and all seem daunting and mighty and overwhelming and it may seem as though one foot paddle and one arm swing at a time won't get us across but that's exactly the prescription. One small movement at a time and don't stop until you get there. So, it doesn't matter if your ocean is fear or alcoholism or addiction. Your ocean may be self-doubt or depression or intolerance. The ocean may be racism or sexism, body image or poverty. Keep swimming. Get to the shore. Your ocean may be following your dreams, going on an adventure, or starting a business. It may take a long time.

When you begin, you may not even see the other side. Have faith, it's there. And when you plant your feet firmly on the shore having completed your goal, raise your weakened arms in victory and know that anything, everything is possible if you're willing to give up the familiarity of comfort and take a chance to get on the other side.

You Can't Expect Whole Love from a Broken Person

I've been talking about lost love quite a bit lately. I have a few friends going through rather painful divorces and breakups. There's been one central theme to the lamentations: why couldn't they love me like I loved them? As I was thinking about the situation of one friend in particular, I said to myself, "You can't expect whole love from a broken person." That person is incapable of giving you what you need. They may try. They may even succeed for a while. Eventually though, if they don't work on themselves, it will not work. It's easy to get caught up when a person does and says all the right things to make you feel good. It's easy to get blinded by the feelings and start to assume your partner is okay. Perhaps they have experienced a life trauma so powerful that they don't know how to genuinely love but have practiced going through the motions long enough to be convincing. Whatever the reason, they have to work on themselves and become a happy and whole person for themselves before they can give one ounce of genuine love to you.

Don't expect other people to fix you.

In the end, we have to practice compassion. We are all made up of broken pieces. We are all beautiful mosaics of shards of pottery, some held together with strong mortar and some incredibly fragile. It's okay to fall in love with the fragile vase, but you cannot get angry when it doesn't hold water. It was never really capable of being what you wanted it to be no matter how beautiful it appeared and no matter how much you wished it were true.

Trust Your Talent

For the past two days, I've been redesigning labels for my packaging. I started the process, not because I needed it, but because I saw another product in a box and I became fixated with the placement of their logo and then I decided after way too much coffee and self-doubt that everything was all wrong about my packaging and I had to fix it. It took me 48 hours to get my mind right and come back to what I already had, although now with a few minor adjustments. I was pretty angry with myself for wasting so much time.

What drew me out of the rabbit hole though, was the realization that I had to stay true to myself. I had to respect my talent enough to know that I had made the right decisions. It's so easy to second-guess ourselves or compare ourselves to other people and then deem ourselves inadequate. The test comes in staying true to ourselves and our own vision. I'm glad I didn't make any radical changes. I want my stationery to be the best representation of my own creative energy. I cannot let anything interfere with that process. Self-doubt is not a friend. Belief in the wisdom of my own talent is what ultimately saved me from wasting more time. I'm okay with the 48 hours of crazy though. Sometimes we need just a little gut check of crazy to remind us that we're already on the right track.

Keep Your Light On

Chasing a dream isn't always the easiest road. Its pavement is broken. There are people on the sidelines cheering for you and against you and sometimes it becomes difficult to decipher who's on which side. It can be lonely. It can be isolating from people who don't understand. But, if it's worth it and if you love it, there are no obstacles too daunting, no dissent too strong, no setback far enough to stop you.

Last night, I talked myself into being pretty depressed thinking about all of things I'd given up in pursuit of a stationery dream. When I felt it coming on, I made myself go to sleep because I knew those thoughts were going to get me nowhere. This morning, I rose with a different perspective. Instead of all the things I'd given up, I thought about all the people who I would have never met had I not started this journey. I think about the events I've helped to shape and the joy I've helped to bring other people and that brings me joy in this moment.

So to the negative thoughts I had last night, I step over you. I'm on a journey and I don't have time to stop to entertain you. There are people and circumstances that will try their damnedest to turn off your light. Sometimes the negativity comes from inside your own mind. But keep your light on. Let it shine. Let it shine. Let it shine.

Done is Better than Perfect

I am a perfectionist and it serves me well in my life, until it doesn't. And what looks like procrastination or unconcern on the outside is actually a frantic search for perfection on the inside. I am learning the art of done. Done doesn't always mean settling for half-ass work. But it does mean that fretting over details that no one will notice but me serves no ultimate purpose in the end. Sometimes done works. I can always fix it later. The world will not end.

Finish it. Move on. Notice a mistake. Fix it. Move on. If everything has to be perfect, then nothing is perfect and nothing gets done.

Learn Your Instrument

I finally watched the documentary *20 Feet from Stardom*. It was mesmerizing and compelling and offered a brief glimpse into the women who created the sounds of revolution. They are the women who sang the hooks and melodies that defined a generation and transformed our culture. And they were largely unsung, unappreciated, and unknown until now. A recurring theme in the documentary is the definition of success. For some, being a background singer is enough. It is a way to travel the world doing what they're good at and make a decent living. For others, the spotlight is the goal. They want to walk that elusive 20 feet. Some make it. Most don't. But, the difference between the good singers, the great singers and the legends is an intimate knowledge of one's own instrument.

Knowledge of one's own instrument, in this case the voice, brings forth a confidence and a freedom to use that voice and stand firm in the beauty it can create be it raw or refined. **A person who is fully in tune to their talent can take risks that others can't.** They can bend notes. They can slide in and out of octaves, modulate with ease. They can play with the dynamics of abandon and control. Those are the people who take our breath away. Those are the people who make us leap to our feet and applaud because we can't believe what we just witnessed. How many of us are truly learning our instruments? How many of us are free to take the creative risks that come along with being confident in who we are and what we can produce? How many of us are doing the absolute best we can with no regard to whether or not anyone will know or even remember our names?

If you want the fruit, take responsibility for the tree.

For over a year, I have been talking to anyone who would listen about wanting to plant fruit trees in my yard. There used to be a peach tree but it's long gone. There's only a pecan tree left. I'd love a citrus grove: oranges, lemon, and grapefruit. I'd also love an avocado tree. Thus far it has been just talk because I keep running through scenarios in my mind of how to maintain them, which varieties should I get, should I buy mature trees or start from seedlings, am I really going to do the work to keep them alive, how do I keep out rodents and on and on and on. All of these thoughts translate to I have not one tree yet.

The bottom line is that I am clear that I don't get the fruit without taking responsibility for the tree. It's fun to focus on the fruit. It's fun to think of being able to walk out into the garden and pick a grapefruit for the morning's breakfast. It's not so much fun checking weather reports to know when to cover them during a freeze, anchoring them so hurricane winds don't topple them before they're developed enough to stand firm on their own, pruning them, mulching them, watering them. That sounds like work. It's also life. We have become a culture where it's desirable to focus on the end result be it wealth, fame, physical appeal, or fruit without having an iota of concern or a plan for the work that goes in beforehand.

I don't know if I'll ever get fruit trees. But rest assured that when I do, they will be well-taken care of because even if they never give me the fruit I want, I made the decision to put them in my yard.

Success is Built in Practice

I watched a fantastic documentary called *Jiro Dreams of Sushi*. When I say, watched, I mean I was mesmerized because I couldn't take my eyes away from the masterful way in which Jiro performs his craft nor could I escape all of the pearls of wisdom he routinely dropped. Apprentices in his kitchen work for ten years before they are ready to work on his line. One of them remarked that Jiro made him make the same egg dish over two-hundred times before he gave his seal of approval! Many would have quit but he persevered. He endured because, as Jiro believes, success is built in practice.

When I first decided to give my life to stationery, I spent over a year, day and night, practicing. I made tons of stationery that never saw the light of day. It was truly one of the best years of my life because I did nothing but practice, learn, and cultivate my style. Because of this time, I don't have to follow every trend. I know who and what I am. I believe wholeheartedly that those who are fans of my work know my style and appreciate it because it doesn't look like everything that's trendy. My success will rise and fall on my constant desire to get better at my craft and to deliver the best that I can every single time to every single customer.

Outward success may be measured in fame, or wealth, or access. But the truly successful is the one who will show up to practice every day, even when no one else is there and who can be counted on to deliver results. That's the long game I'm playing to win.

About the Author

Angel Robinson has been writing this book since she was 15 years old. It was then she began the daily practice of journaling. Writing everyday about her life, her thoughts, and her reactions to events, forced her to become a good listener and to consciously evaluate all of the information, advice, and life lessons that came her way. She began her career in government after earning a Master's Degree in Urban and Regional Planning. Combined with her undergraduate work in Sociology and Psychology, Angel is constantly interested in exploring why things happen, not just the sequence of events. She changed careers after experiencing immeasurable loss during Hurricane Katrina and was forced to relocate to Texas. She decided to follow her ultimate passion of designing stationery and opened the online shop, Write Robinson. She then returned to her hometown of New Orleans and continues to pursue her dreams. In addition, she is the co-founder and Creative Director of Grey Buddha, a design and business branding firm. This book is her first published work.

Made in the USA
Columbia, SC
15 July 2017